SINGLE
&WHOLE

RHENA TAYLOR

D1403096

INTERVARSITY PRESS
DOWNERS GROVE, ILLINOIS 60515

Copyright © Rhena Taylor 1984

Published in the United States of America by InterVarsity Press, Downers Grove, Illinois, with permission from Kingsway Publications Ltd., Eastbourne, England. Published in England under the title Every Single Blessing.

All rights reserved. No part of this book may be reproduced in any form without written permission from InterVarsity Press, Downers Grove, Ilinois.

InterVarsity Press is the book-publishing division of Inter-Varsity Christian Fellowship, a student movement active on campus at hundreds of universities, colleges and schools of nursing. For information about local and regional activities, write IVCF, 233 Langdon St., Madison, WI 53703.

Unless otherwise stated, biblical quotations are from the Revised Standard Version, copyrighted 1946, 1952, © 1971, 1973 by the Division of Christian Education of the National Council of the Churches of Christ in the USA.

Cover photograph: David Singer

ISBN 0-87784-510-7

Printed in the United States of America

Library of Congress Cataloguing in Publication Data
Taylor, Rhena.
  Single and whole.

  1. Single people—Religious life.   2. Taylor, Rhena.
I. Title.
BV4596.S5T38   1985   248.8′4   85-8345
ISBN 0-87784-510-7

| 16 | 15 | 14 | 13 | 12 | 11 | 10 | 9 | 8 | 7 | 6 | 5 | 4 | 3 | 2 | 1 |
| 97 | 96 | 95 | 94 | 93 | 92 | 91 | 90 | 89 | 88 | 87 | 86 | 85 | | | |

1 The Gift of Singleness

I used to say that there were two days in the year when I minded not being married: Christmas eve and Christmas day. And yet it was on one Christmas eve that, for almost the first time, I understood something about the single state and myself.

I was in England for Christmas and staying with my parents. We had decided to go to the Christmas eve carol service in Norwich Cathedral. My younger brother and his wife came with us and I drove the family car and parked it near the Cathedral. It was a cold, clear night and the moon which was rising above the Cathedral buildings was brilliant and beautiful. Snuggled into each other, my parents walked towards the Cathedral West door followed by my brother and his wife. I delayed, locking the car doors, and then followed alone.

The scene is etched in my memory as I followed those two couples, for it was the traditional time for me to feel my lack of a partner: someone to snuggle into on this cold night! And yet I did not. Watching them I was glad for them, for both were good marriages. But I was glad for me, too: alone, free and happy in the Lord. It was as right and as blessed for me to walk alone that night as it was for them to have each other.

Of course I caught up with them in a moment but before I had registered that feeling of exulting in the gift of singleness, a state in which close fellowship with God, single-minded devotion to his service and love of his people can reach heights often denied to the married.

This is not perhaps most people's view of the single life: but it is a biblical one.

'I want you to be free from anxieties,' writes the apostle Paul in 1 Corinthians 7. 'The unmarried man is anxious about the affairs of the Lord, how to please the Lord; but the married man is anxious about worldly affairs, how to please his wife, and his interests are divided. And the unmarried woman or girl is anxious about the affairs of the Lord, how to be holy in body and spirit; but the married woman is anxious about worldly affairs, how to please her husband. I say this for your own benefit... to secure your undivided devotion to the Lord.'

What was Paul saying here? He says that the single person can have an undivided aim in life: to please the Lord; whereas the married will often be struggling with two aims in life: to please the Lord and also to keep their marriage together. There seems little doubt that, to Paul, the state of singleness for a Christian had a lot to recommend it.

That being so, I find myself wondering why, in over thirty years now as a Christian, I have never heard a minister of God preach on singleness as a good option for a Christian. I have sat through sermon after sermon on marriage but I have never heard a recommendation for the single state even though the pews have been filled with single people.

Of course the Bible commentaries on 1 Corinthians 7 tend to lessen its impact by pointing out that Paul was caught up in the increasing persecution of the early church and was expecting Christ to return imminently. It was, we are told, the situation in which he found himself that caused him to encourage the single state.

But what is the situation in which we find ourselves today? Is the return of the Lord any less imminent? Is there any less need for 'undivided devotion' to the Lord in our troubled and frightened world of the twentieth century?

Could it be, I wonder, that the Western church has glorified marriage to such an extent that men and women who are truly called to the single state cannot stand up against the cultural and social emphases in society and so marry out of God's will? And, if that is so, what responsibility for that must be borne by the ministry of our Western church?

Certainly, as I have observed rocking Christian marriages, children separated for years from their missionary parents, and wives and husbands who appear to be crippled spiritually through their partner's inadequacies, I have wondered whether more people are called to singleness in the Christian world than have the courage to accept that calling.

If this book is being read by the married I can hear

them saying at this point: 'But of course the single state is an acceptable one for the Christian. Does anyone deny it? Why write a book about it? Isn't that, in itself, casting doubt on the matter?'

But most single people in the church today won't respond like that. They have lived too long with:

'Don't give up hope, my dear. The Lord will bring the right man along in his time.'

'But you *can't* be a missionary! You'll never get married that way.'

'Why don't you go on one of those singles holidays? I hear there are a lot of unattached males on those.'

'Dear, I want you to come to dinner on Tuesday. I've rather an interesting person I want you to meet...'

The implication of all such remarks is, of course, that the single state is one that everyone wants to get out of as quickly as possible.

Often I have even found books on the subject deeply depressing, with their brave attempt at assuring me that I might get to *like* being single; their comment (in a tone of disbelief) that some people see being single as a gift from God; and their pages of advice about what to do ('Start a Bible study or prayer group in your home', 'Take up a hobby', 'Enjoy children. Children like the visitor who talks with them, tells them stories, or teaches them a song') and what not to do ('Don't stay talking to the husband while the wife is washing up in the kitchen').

Such advice may well be excellent but it tends to side-step the real issue, for surely this attitude of 'making the best of things' is not the only one for the single to have? Isn't there something more: something far more fulfilling, joyous and rewarding?

Jesus said he came to give us abundant life (Jn 10:10) and throughout the Epistles and in the Old Testament there are many descriptions of the people of God as joyful, victorious and fulfilled people: 'filled with all the fulness of God' (Eph 3:19). We are 'fellow citizens with the saints and members of the household of God' (Eph 2:19). We are sons and daughters of a King (Jn 1:12). Study the Bible. Get a picture of the man of God who is 'like a tree planted by water, that sends out its roots by the stream and does not fear when heat comes, for its leaves remain green' (Jer 17:8). Get a picture of the Lord who, in Christ, 'always leads us in triumph, and through us spreads the fragrance of the knowledge of him everywhere' (2 Cor 2:14). And then ask yourself: are these glorious proud promises not for you? Do these pictures of the blessed, fruitful and triumphant Christian refer only to those who are married? You are reading odd things into the Bible if you think that!

About eighteen years ago I was a very young missionary. The death of my mother had brought me home after only a year and a half in Ethiopia and I had been invited to attend a 'mission orientation' weekend for recruits. I would, it was implied, be able to share with them what the first year abroad was *really* like.

They were being addressed by an older, married, missionary doctor. He was speaking on being single overseas.

'To be a single woman in Africa today is to be

subject to a great many stresses and strains,' he told the group in which single women predominated. 'You must be prepared to face loneliness and frustration and you will almost certainly not be understood by African society. Your relationship with the married men on your station may be a continual problem.'

He want on in this strain for some time and then called on me to corroborate what he had said.

'I ... er ... I don't think it's that much of a problem,' I said nervously, for he was a 'big man' in the Society and I did not like to disagree with him.

'Then you must be unlike most young women!' was the curt answer, which effectively destroyed any credibility I might have had with the group and created in me a feeling that I wasn't really being honest and probably was abnormal in some way, if not totally undersexed.

We did not discuss the matter further at that conference but it is strange that I remember the occasion so well. Maybe that experience has had something to do with the fact that though, over the years, I have often counselled and helped people who were finding singleness a problem, I have never spoken of it in public or written anything on it until last year: my twentieth as a missionary.

I was visiting Addis Ababa as a lecturer in Communications and was asked, as a side-line, to take some missionary orientation lectures for the Norwegian mission. One of the subjects given me was 'the single woman missionary'. It was not a title I would have chosen myself but I saw no special reason for refusing the topic, so one afternoon in my little house in Addis Ababa, I settled down to prepare for the session.

It was the first time I had tried to collect my thoughts clearly concerning singleness in the Christian life: the first time I had set down on paper anything about it. And as I did so, I was surprised by joy. I began to see so clearly that singleness had been the Lord's gift to me: the open door to so much I had never before expressed openly. It was as if a married woman, preparing a talk on the blessing of marriage, found herself re-living with joy all the precious moments of her marriage. I found myself re-living with joy all the precious moments of singleness. Perhaps it was that afternoon in Addis Ababa that was the real forerunner of this book: the moment that summed up my feelings and experiences over the years concerning the gift of singleness.

2 Self-Worth and the Single Life

People who meet me for the first time very often have problems in relating to me. Later on, when they get closer to me, they usually at some point say, 'You know, I never thought you were like this. The first time I met you I thought you were....' Well, the adjectives differ, but they are rarely complimentary!

I'm getting such a hang-up about this now that I don't let people finish the sentence.

'I understand you, Rhena,' said an older colleague to me a year or so ago. 'I realize that the selfconfidence you appear to have is just a front. Inside you're just as timid and fearful as the rest of us.'

For some years I have agreed meekly with this assessment without making much comment. In a way I have genuinely accepted it. It is clearly 'up to date' to believe we all are wearing masks to hide our real selves. Yes, probably this confidence I appear to others to have is 'just a front'. But, more recently, I have begun to question that. *Is* it a 'mask'? Am I just 'making the best of things'? Deep down inside me, is there a shrinking, fearful little miserable self that's sort of covered over with layers of something called confidence that might slide off in times of stress?

But I find it is rather the opposite.

'Let him who boasts, boast of the Lord,' said Paul (2 Cor 10:17). And as I write this paragraph it is of him I am thinking. Inside me (that is, as far down as I have managed to get!) there is a solid core of confidence in Jesus as the Saviour of my soul and the director of my destiny. I have known him in my life since I was fourteen and I believe he is guiding me throughout my life to make right decisions. I love him and I belong to him. He is—despite my best efforts to the contrary!—teaching me how to live for him in this life, and shaping me to live with him in eternity. This gives me confidence even when people appear to reject or abuse me. I believe that I am safe in his hand and that I will continue to be safe as long as I genuinely try to obey him and trust him.

This doesn't, of course, give me confidence in all the peripheral areas of my life. I'm as cowardly as the next man (woman!) when it comes to complaining to the milkman that I have been overcharged. I'm horrified if someone leaves me with a baby under a year old or asks me to look after her potted plants. I go through agonies waiting for an editor to give me an opinion on something I've written and I get furious at other people's weighing machines. Yes, there are numerous areas in life where I lack confidence, but they are not deep ones. Underneath I have a strong sense of self-worth as a child of God.

Now for a single person this question of confidence is very important for, as I have already indicated, it is

13

amazing how often such confidence in our self-worth is shaken by well-meaning friends and relations.

'Don't give up hope,' says your married friend periodically. 'I had a friend who got married for the first time when she was nearly sixty and is blissfully happy!'

Yes: the society we live in certainly tends to push us into viewing every unattached male as a potential husband. The single woman should go to evening classes in electrical engineering, take great pains with her appearance, and try not to contradict the male sex!

But when we live the single life with that attitude we express a deep dissatisfaction with the way things are, and it in no way helps us to acquire the sense of self-worth which I am talking about.

As a missionary beginning to get involved in literature work, I once met a single woman missionary in her thirties who had for some years successfully edited a Christian magazine in one of the African countries. I had known her work for some years and admired it. She had recently announced her engagement to an older Christian man and was glowing with happiness.

'You know,' she said to me confidentially. 'All those years when I was working on the magazine, I felt certain there would be an end to it some day when I would find real joy.'

I can remember now the sense of shock with which I heard her say that. She had had an interesting and fruitful job; was that how she regarded it—as simply the years during which she waited for her 'real life' to begin? Was that kind of 'half life' all a Christian could expect in the years before marriage? And what if they didn't marry? Would they be in a state of 'waiting' for ever?

I also remember a well-known Christian leader addressing a seminar on the subject of singleness at a charismatic conference. He was explaining that of *course* single people had a place in the church of God. It might, he said with a smile, be difficult to find that place ('When they come to stay, where do you put them? In the back bedroom with the children?') but the married must welcome them and help them. 'There is,' he declared, 'in every single person a touch of the adolescent. They have never quite grown up.'

I wonder if he had remembered that Jesus was single.

Confidence. A sense of self-worth. If we do find it as single people, it certainly isn't without some discouragement from the married, some of whom seem almost threatened by the idea that fulfilment in life can lie outside marriage as well as within it.

Is an unmarried person somehow less of a person than the married? Can they be called 'not quite grown up'?

The secular world, at least in the West, does not seem to suffer greatly from such concepts. In the secular world, the single woman is seen as a woman who has made an (often sensible) choice against marriage and the single man is almost congratulated at having 'escaped the net'. For either sex, the social stigma of virginity is simply removed by living with someone for a while.

No, it is in the Christian church that singleness causes unhappiness. At a time when the Gospel is being presented in the traditional churches in a way that seems to attract more women than men, the church teaches that marriage is for life and should be with a fellow believer. Consequently it is the Christian woman who collapses on your settee and tells you that she cannot face life unmarried, not the non-Christian. And that may well be an indictment against a church that is so slow to teach on the gift of singleness.

The promises in the Bible which lead us to expect that Christians can and should live joyful and fulfilled lives are not linked in any way with the married state. 'Ye are complete in him,' says the Authorized Version of Colossians 2:10. The Revised Standard Version gives it as 'You have come to fulness of life in him'. How can such an important matter as whether or not someone is a 'whole person' be dependent on their outward circumstances? All that we need to make us complete and fulfilled in life can be ours through Christ. It does not depend on whether or not we are married, healthy, employed, good-looking or highly-educated! Full power to live the 'life abundant' promised by Christ is a possibility for every child of God: married, single, divorced, separated or widowed!

3 God's Best

'Why aren't you married?'

I have been asked that question by old countrymen in Ethiopia, business executives in Kenya, fellow-students in America and a wide variety of people in England.

What I say depends on the mood of the moment:

'I never had the time.'

'I never wanted to.'

'Because I was interested in my career.'

'I didn't like the men who asked me.'

More recently, rather harassed in a demanding job in Kenya, I have said shortly, 'Because I need a wife not a husband!'

But if I am asked this by a fellow Christian in an atmosphere where a serious answer is required, there is really only one answer to this question and I give it: 'Singleness is the state to which God has called me.'

Singleness is God's *best* for me.

I realize that to some lonely, panic-stricken women (and perhaps men) this answer might not ring true. How could singleness be God's *best* for anyone? I have already answered this question in the two earlier chapters. I sincerely believe that there is a place for the unmarried in the perfect will of God, a calling to the single life, and that God has chosen men and women to fill it. I also believe widows, widowers, separated and divorced Christians who are truly trying to follow the will of God in their lives belong in that calling.

It is important not only to say this but to believe it. If you are a Christian who sincerely wants the will of God in your life, then you are not single (or alone) because you:

— went to a women's teachers' training college;
— belong to the war generation;
— are unattractive and perhaps too strong-willed;
— are confined to your home looking after mother;
— never meet any men;
— have had your partner cruelly taken away by God;
— are neglected by your children.

You are single because it is God's calling and choice for you at this time. His chosen ministry for you now is that of a single person.

Even as the gift of marriage can be for five years or fifty, so the gift of singleness may not be for ever. Statistically, most women marry. The gift of single-ness that I am talking about belongs as much to the girl of twenty as to the woman of forty. The gift of singleness can even be returned to the woman of sixty whose husband has died after thirty years of happy married life. To all who are Christians and who are single or living alone at this moment, I would say the same thing: singleness is the state to which God has called you. Singleness is God's *best* for you.

Now I may sound a little unrealistic here. I can well imagine what sort of reception you'd get if you went to a grieving widow and told her to rejoice because she has really had the gift of singleness given back to her! Of course there is an agonizing period to go through if you have lost a much-loved partner of many years. But as the pain gradually eases you do have an option: either to live in the past or to accept the present and believe in the future. There is nothing in the Bible about a Christian retiring. Rather, he 'does not cease to bear fruit' (Jer 17:8, and also Psalm 92:12–14). And the fact that you are suddenly alone can alter, but need not wither up, your ministry.

I know an English widow living abroad who lost her husband suddenly after a long and happy marriage. She was shattered by it, liable to burst into tears when his name was mentioned, a compulsive worker and unable to stay happily alone in her house. But as the years passed, she began to adjust. Not quickly, but steadily. She took a new place in society and saw a new ministry. She has a gift of insight into people and situations that is given to very few and also has the gift of being able to encourage and exhort God's servants. And she uses those gifts. Her ministry is real and fruitful; but it is a different one, the one of a single person.

To those experiencing it, singleness is a calling from God: his perfect will for you. It is no mistake. Can you believe that? If you can, you're on the way to achieving that confidence and sense of self-worth

19

which will stand you in good stead whether you are married or single. And to those who commiserate with your singleness in a way which makes you feel deprived and rejected you can say: 'Why challenge God's choice for my life? Is your plan for me better than his?'

Yes, the sovereign will of God is of great importance to me. I do not think the Creator of an infinite universe with its intricate planning and order has anything but an ordered plan for each child of his. One perfect will. One ministry.

'My sheep hear my voice,' said Jesus, 'and they follow me' (Jn 10:27). That doesn't mean wandering all over the place but following the Lord within his perfect will. Only by deliberate rejection of that will can we find ourselves away from that leadership and even then repentance can bring us back into it.

This makes the question of guidance, of course, of paramount importance. The problems of guidance demand a book in themselves and do not belong in this book. But I sincerely believe that if we honestly give the Lord open options in our lives and don't put conditions on our service ('Yes, Lord, anywhere for you but, please, not a parish in the north of England!'), he will not let us make mistakes. God does not deliberately make guidance difficult, though *we* might. He does not play games with us: he wants us in his way.

Perhaps I should make one comment here, however, on the subject of following the Lord. I think no Christian will follow him very far without realizing his liking for acting at what seems to us to be the last minute. As a missionary who has moved around quite a bit I have grown resigned, if not always very cheerful, about it! It is obviously of importance to the Lord that we learn to trust him even in situations where there appear no grounds for doing so. Accordingly he very often asks us to wait *his* timing rather than arranging things according to ours.

This is, of course, not directly related to the subject of singleness: we all experience this tendency of the Lord to ask us to wait, trusting in him, until the light turns green. How long had Abraham to wait for the fulfilling of God's promise? How long did David wait for his kingdom? How long did Moses care for sheep in the wilderness before the Lord allowed him to lead the Israelites out of Egypt? How long did the prophets wait for the promised Messiah? And how long do we, in the smaller affairs in our life, have to wait for God to lead us on? Sometimes we wait until it seems impossible for God to answer our prayers.

When Sarah reached the age of not bearing children, do you think she didn't notice it? 'Lord, my *periods are going to stop* and you still haven't given me a child!'

And how often I have said in despair: 'Lord, tomorrow is the *last possible day* for getting that visa. I'll never get to teach that course at all if it doesn't come.'

Or: 'Lord, *why* haven't they written by now to let me know about that job? I'm just wasting time here.'

Or: 'Lord, I really have to have that money by *tomorrow* or I don't know what to do.'

Or: 'Lord, surely the Board has made *some* kind of decision on that matter by *now*!'

And so on. Do you hear yourself?

Yes, the Lord waits: to our 'last minute' and beyond it, but the thing is done. Yes, we beat on the closed doors that face us, but when the Lord wants to open them they fly open to the touch.

I have experienced this all my Christian life and though I still, in the weakness of the flesh, put my shoulder to those closed doors, yet in my heart of hearts I know his way is best and can wait for him. It's a beautiful promise in Isaiah 49:23: 'I am the Lord...those who wait for me shall not be put to shame.'

In 1975 I had to leave Ethiopia. I returned to England with no idea what to do next except that I felt I needed further training in Communications and thought I might get it in the USA. So I started to make plans and everything went so slowly! Letters took weeks instead of days (I'm not even sure there wasn't a postal strike somewhere around), forms were wrongly filled in, references took a long time in coming. The first quarter came and went and I was still hanging around at home. Then the January term started. ('Lord, if I can't make it now I'll have to wait to next September and the Mission will never buy that.')

The right form actually came ten days after the start of the January quarter and in the end I landed in the USA two weeks late for my first quarter in an American Graduate School (what was a 'quarter' anyway?), in the biggest snow storm Chicago had experienced all winter. But I found that a set of rooms had been vacated by a leaving student the day before I got there and that I was about the only new international graduate student not in trouble about finding digs.

Yes, the Lord's timing is best. I know that from many many experiences, and I trust him. But get used to last minute action if you want to make a success of following the Lord. It's just the way he does things. I understand better now the reference in Hebrews to those who 'through faith *and patience* inherit the promises' (Heb 6:12)!

And also get used to the fact that there will be suffering, for being in the perfect will of God does not mean that we escape suffering, in fact it may increase it.

'Can he have followed far,' wrote Amy Carmichael, 'who has nor wound, nor scar?' (Amy Carmichael, 'No Scar', *Toward Jerusalem*, SPCK 1936).

Satan is the one referred to as the 'ruler of this world', not Christ (Jn 14:30). But God, who watches over his children on earth with 'loving kindness and tender mercy', does not allow us to suffer more than we can bear: and somehow manages to fold that suffering into his plan for us on earth, part of making us more like Christ, more fit for Eternity.

But singleness does not come in this category of 'allowed evil'. If we suffer just because of our single state, then it is often our pride that is suffering and we are demonstrating both to God and to the world around us that we cannot trust him to order our lives for us. It is our inability to accept the Lord's will in our lives, our earthly priorities, that is causing that suffering, not God, who, if we let him, will lead us into a fruitful and fulfilled ministry. We either believe honestly that 'he is able to keep that which I have committed unto him' (2 Tim 1:12 av) or we don't.

Recently I was at a school sports day. A little boy, perhaps about seven, was running in the egg-and-spoon race. Watching his agonized concentration and intense effort brought tears to my eyes. He was at the front of the field—five yards away from the winning tape—two yards—and then tragedy: he tripped on a tussock and fell. The race was won by someone else and a sympathetic teacher helped him up. He was crying. So was I!

What makes one cry at such times? It is the sight of so much agony, so much importance, given to so trivial a thing. You long to call out to the child, 'But it doesn't matter. Don't you see, it doesn't matter!' His mother will tell him that, of course, but that doesn't help at the moment. At that moment his world is in ruins.

I have a feeling that when we suffer on this earth not because of sin (which is a little different) but because of something we cannot honestly help, then God might be wanting to call out to us the same thing... 'It doesn't matter. Don't you see it doesn't matter?'

We are called by God on this earth to join battle against the powers of evil and to call others into the Kingdom of God. When Christians are really conscious of this (in lands, for example, where they are being persecuted) the question of whether they happen to be married or single is of very little importance. I have sometimes felt that the whole of our

Christian life on this planet is as if we are missionaries sent from heaven for about seventy or eighty years. Maybe when we get back to heaven we'll have a sort of de-briefing on our service here, rather like the missionary who goes back to his sending church after completing his term of service in Africa or Asia. Maybe the angels will say: 'Hey, you were one of those chosen missionaries in that sin-ruled earth, weren't you? How did it go?'

If we could get our life on this earth into that sort of perspective the question of marriage as against singleness might sink into some insignificance.

It doesn't matter. Don't you see it doesn't matter?

4 Pro-Marriage

A book that had quite an effect on my life was a small one called *Love Is a Feeling to Be Learned* by Walter Trobisch (IVP 1971). Among other things, it introduced me to the idea that 'the desire to be married is the condition for a happy single life.'

That was helpful to me at the time because one of my friends, an attractive woman in the mid-thirties, had been saying, 'I don't want to get married.' She was not one I would have described as a 'career woman' and somehow the remark did not ring true. Although I hadn't spent a lot of time thinking about the matter, I did have a kind of feeling that the way to happiness in the single life was not by basing it on a lie. To 'kid ourselves' that really marriage isn't what we wanted after all, does not seem to me a very positive approach.

Now I may sound as if I am contradicting all I have said up to now about believing that singleness is a calling from God, and not spending all our time waiting for the moment of marriage. But there is a difference between regarding marriage as the only possible option in life, and understanding that it is the normal way of life for the majority of people. No single person can afford to be *anti-marriage* either for others or for themselves. I would, I suppose, make an exception here for those who feel it right to commit themselves to vows of lifetime celibacy, but for most people I think it is quite important to say, 'Yes, I would rather have been married and I will be open to the possibility of marriage at any time if the Lord leads me that way', before talking about the gift of singleness. We do need to acknowledge to ourselves and to others that marriage is the norm for the Christian and singleness the exception, if only to see more clearly some of the 'exceptional' things open to single people!

Following that recognition should come a will-ingness to accept the Lord's choice for us and an awareness that no one's life, married or single, is quite what they want it to be. Perfection does not exist this side of eternity. If we are to live realistically on this earth we have to know that, accept it, and go on living just the same. 'The task we have to face is the same whether we are married or single,' writes Trobisch, 'to live a fulfilled life in spite of many unfulfilled desires.'

I understand that honeymoons are sometimes not all they are made out to be. 'There was really nothing to do on our honeymoon but walk around a golf course holding hands,' said one young wife to me. 'I thought to myself that if this was marriage, I could have done without it!' Yes, the gift of marriage, though accepted as God's will by two young people, might well take some time to be appreciated.

So the gift of singleness may not be greatly appreciated at first by the twentieth-century product of western society who has been conditioned to believe that not to 'get your man' signals personal and social disaster.

I learned a lot of new phrases while in the States. One of them was the expression 'senior panic'. It describes the mental state of college girls who reach their last year at college without having formed a steady relationship with a man. Panic! Agony! There'll never be so many Christian men together again! I'll never get married!

It takes a strong Christian character to stand out against that sort of pressure.

Jesus, living in a society in which marriage was honoured and expected, recognized that singleness as a calling would not be culturally acceptable to many people.

> The disciples said to him, "If such is the case of a man with his wife, it is not expedient to marry." But he said to them, "Not all men can receive this precept, but only those to whom it is given. For there are eunuchs who have been so from birth, and there are eunuchs who have been made eunuchs by men and there are eunuchs who have made themselves eunuchs for the sake of the kingdom of Heaven. He who is able to receive this, let him receive it" (Mt 19:10—11).

This is as clear a statement as I have seen in the Bible that the state of singleness may be pretty difficult to understand or accept in some societies.

It is because I recognize this, that I do not appreciate jokes about the unmarried. Singleness causes too much suffering for me to see it as funny when people are single.

'Not "old maids", my dear,' says the Vicar genially. 'Unclaimed blessings. That's what *I* say.' Ha ha.

'We've put you in that row of rooms up there. We call it the hen house,' says the missionary running the Mission guest house. You smile feebly.

I remember moving into a new house in Addis Ababa with two other single ladies. The mission leader, helping us move, began referring to the house as 'the spinney', a play on the word 'spinster'. I let it go for a while, hoping he'd forget it. Then we had a straight talk. Either he stopped using that phrase or he would not be welcome in our home. He was a gracious man and the matter ended there.

'Love is a feeling to be learned.' It was, and is, a lovely phrase.

The gift of singleness needs love to let it operate successfully just as much as marriage does.

'What is an old maid?' asks Trobisch. 'Someone unable to love. Someone who represses his feelings and doesn't say yes to himself. There are teenage "old maids". There are also married "old maids". There are even male "old maids"'! (From *Love Is a Feeling to Be Learned*.)

For all Christians, love is going to be central to the matter of living a happy and fulfilled life. 'We need more faith, more unity, more prayer,' we say in our empty churches. Do we? Or do we need to learn more about love?

'Do not lay up for yourselves treasures on earth, where moth and rust consume and where thieves break in and steal,' said Jesus, 'but lay up for yourselves treasures in heaven...' (Mt 6:19, 20). What are those 'treasures in heaven'? Not, I fear, the sermons we have preached, the meetings we have attended, the courses we have organized, even the books we have published. I think they might be the love-relationships that we have formed and the actions (such as those listed in Matthew 25:35) that are a result of those love-relationships.

We learn from 1 Corinthians 3:12 that it is possible to build upon the foundation of our belief in Christ, works of gold, silver, and precious stones, or works of wood, hay and stubble. Obviously one set of works will last and one will not. What's the difference? I think it might be the extent to which love is mixed up in those works. I don't know that it matters greatly whether or not what we have done has been enormously successful. It does matter whether or not we did it in the right spirit.

It is love which makes a work of hay and wood become a work of silver and gold. It is love that starts us on that pile of treasure in heaven. It is love which transforms what might be a dry and embittered life into one both radiant and fruitful.

Love is a feeling to be learned.

5 The Ministry of Love

One of the difficulties about committing yourself to a printed page is that your opinion about things changes, but what you write stays the same. In an earlier book, written after some eight years abroad, I wrote:

> One must "love the people". One had read it in all the best missionary classics. But I cannot express the relief with which I once read in some magazine or book, "Love the people? How can I love such a vague indeterminate mass? Why should I be expected to love Indians or Africans in a different way from the way in which I love my own countrymen? I love *people* not "the people". I love some. I find others difficult to love. I admire some, I dislike or pity others. They are exactly the same to me as are my friends and acquaintances in England. As a Christian, I pray that God will give me a love for them all—all that I know, but I don't go around with my heart bursting with love for all I see." Now I drew a great breath of relief when I read that: because at last someone had been honest enough to say it! (Helen Morgan, *Who'd Stay a Missionary?* Patmos Press 1971.)

That was obviously true for me at the time of writing but it is not true for me now. I am finding out that there *is* a kind of 'blanket love' for people available to the Christian: a love that operates for my friends and my colleagues, yes, but which can also operate for a short time to a lonely, frightened elderly man pouring out his worries on Waterloo station, or to a nervous and blustering adolescent sure that he has all the answers to life already. It is a love that appears the moment someone faces me, and it has little, if anything, to do with how that person is feeling towards me.

How does such a love come? There is only one answer to that: it comes 'because God's love has been poured into our hearts through the Holy Spirit which has been given to us' (Rom 5:5). It comes through the Holy Spirit.

I belong to the generation of Christians in England who really got 'short-changed' on the subject of the Holy Spirit! I was carefully nurtured as a young Christian by Scripture Union notes, Crusader Bible study courses, and all the right books, camps and conferences. I still grew into an adult with no idea that the Holy Spirit was more than a kind of ghostly influence which had some functions in my life like 'comforting' me and teaching me to pray 'with sighs that cannot be uttered'. Possibly this lack of understanding was because I couldn't imagine him (it?). 'Father' and the 'Son' both have human equivalents. But what is the 'human equivalent' of the Holy Spirit: a white, indistinct figure that comes out at night?

Anyway, when I was in Ethiopia the charismatic

renewal was beginning to be seen there, initially among some Ethiopian school boys, and it swept me along with it. Despite the initial very wary reaction of my Mission society, my identification with the 'charismatics' as they were beginning to be called, did not result (as it did with some societies) in my being asked to leave the society. And so I was left to discover the Holy Spirit.

And it was joy: a whole part of the character of God I had never known before: a new 'Person' and one, moreover, who was deeply and vitally interested in me and my poor efforts at living the Christian life. The Sanctifier. Yes, I had loved God my Father and Jesus my Saviour for many years but what had I known of God the Holy Spirit? It was like having a new friend, a new confidant, a new counsellor. I sometimes prayed to him alone—'Lord Spirit'—a habit I have maintained ever since.

I do not recall at that time any special thrilling experience, although I did begin to speak in tongues, but what I do remember is that the feeling I had had for years that I was missing out on something in my spiritual life, just disappeared. And although there have been plenty of ups and downs in my spiritual life since then, that feeling never returned and I now feel with Peter that, though I might not always demonstrate the fact, 'His divine power has granted to me *all things* that pertain to life and godliness' (2 Pet 1:3).

To what extent the love growing inside me had its root with the experience mentioned above, I don't know: but certainly it has come in the years since.

And if it is not always visible to others, that is how far I still live solidly in the flesh rather than in the spirit! At any rate, I believe now that spiritual love for others does exist through the Holy Spirit, and that it can soften and mould us into loving people in a way nothing else can.

Many years ago I read a book by Hannah Hurnard called *Hinds' Feet on High Places* (Christian Literature Crusade 1955). It is a spiritual allegory in which her 'heroine', Much Afraid, travels to the 'high places'. Towards the end of the book there was an incident that puzzled me and, perhaps because of that, remained in my mind for some time. Much Afraid was led to a 'grave in the mountains' where she was asked to sacrifice the 'natural, human love' that was in her heart. That really intrigued me. Surely to learn to love is what we are seeking as Christians? What could be the matter with 'natural, human love'? And yet, over the years, I have begun to see what might be the matter with it.

Natural, human love is limited to our family and those we call our friends. It can be possessive and demanding and looks for love in return. Spiritual love (of the kind talked about in 1 Corinthians 13) simply offers itself freely to all. It is ready to let go. It is not dependent on the response of the loved. It is God's type of love, that he offers to the world he created. It is ours through his Holy Spirit.

I cannot see natural love as wrong in itself but I can see that it might lead to wrong doing, whereas spiritual love will not. To love someone is to desire their highest good at whatever the cost to yourself.

There are times when natural love will rise to those heights and then it is a foreshadowing of spiritual love but, it only foreshadows, for it is not truly the fruit of the Spirit.

But natural love may be a springboard to God's love. It is often through the love of an earthly father that a child first begins to understand the love of a heavenly father. Perhaps, for some, it is love for a husband or wife that is the first intimation of the love which Jesus gives us through the Spirit. After all, the New Testament is full of parallels between the love of husband and wife and the love of Christ for the church (e.g. Eph 5:21–33). Consequently, even as a child with a violent and drunken father might find it hard to comprehend the love of God as his Father, so one who has not experienced natural love might find it harder to go on to finding out the joys of spiritual love.

This might relate to singleness. Perhaps it is more difficult for the single person to find this spiritual love, or even to realize it is there. Certainly there seem to be love-less lives around us sometimes!

But this love of God that can be poured into our hearts through the Holy Spirit is available equally for all: dependent on nothing except our openness to receive it. And once the single person has understood that this love is possible and has found the source of it, then I believe he or she has a ministry of love to offer, greater in scope than the ministry of the married.

I was once asked by my Mission to write down my 'aims and priorities' in life. I did so. I saw my first responsibility as being directly to the Lord, to be obedient to his will. My second was to the body of Christ and my service in it. My third was to the organization in which I was then working. Commenting on these my (African) boss remarked, 'Yes, I think these are good. Of course I would put responsibility to my wife and children in between your number one and two.'

I remembered that. Basically it said to me that in our relationship *he* would always be more important to *me* than *I* would be to *him*. As a member of the body of Christ, he was my second priority, but I was his third. Now I do not disagree with my boss here. I understand that his responsibility to care for the family God has given him is important and right. But it did make a difference to me. And the fact that the single person has no immediate family to care for does mean very often that others can get closer to them, just because there is more room close to their hearts. And there are an awful lot of people in the world today who want and need that room! It is possible for single people to understand much more about the true meaning of the family of God than some married people: because their earthly family does not claim their first attention.

It was Jesus—a single man—who showed us the reality of the family of God.

While he was still speaking to the people, behold, his mother and his brothers stood outside, asking to speak to him. But he replied to the man who told him, "Who is my mother, and who are my brothers?" And stretching out his hand toward his disciples he said, "Here are my mother and my brothers! For whoever does the will of my Father in heaven is my brother, and sister, and mother" (Mt 12:46–50).

Had Jesus been married and his wife and children 'standing outside' then perhaps he would not have given that answer: a sufficiently good reason perhaps for him not to have married!

But we are talking about love, and remember this: 'the measure you give will be the measure you get' (Mt 7:2). Although you may not be loved back by the person to whom you offer your love, love *will* return to you. It snowballs.

I have not been a missionary for more than twenty years without at times wishing I had more money. But I notice that if I keep giving, so I keep receiving. Not from the same people, of course, but it does return to me. In the same way, if I keep my home always open to offer hospitality, then, when I need a home, homes open to me.

'The measure you give will be the measure you get.'

'To him that hath shall be given.'

Try it and see!

6 The Tenth Person

I wonder by now if you are beginning to think that I operate on a different plane from you: that this idea of going around loving everyone sounds all right but just isn't an option for most ordinary people? Well, this chapter and the next will tell you that, sadly, my feet are planted pretty firmly on this earth. Plenty of things get in the way of my loving everyone and if *I* have made it through to discovering at least the beginning of this love in my heart, so can you!

'All very well, her talking about learning to love people,' you're saying. 'She hasn't got a mother like mine—colleague like mine—neighbour like mine (yes, even)—vicar like mine!'

Haven't I? Do you think there is no one in my life that I look at and wonder if I'll ever get to love? Do you think I don't recognize that there are some quite large boggy patches and rather nasty precipices in this whole business of learning to love each other?

When I had been a missionary (yes, a *missionary*, one of those holy 'set-apart' people!) for over ten years, I was nearly thrown out of the mission on the question of my bad personal relationships with my fellow missionaries.

The trouble was that I have never reacted well to missionaries in a group. One by one, even two by two, they are great people, but put them together and I get bristly and defensive immediately. This meant I never gave much attention to my relationship within the mission group in Addis Ababa. I had to go to mission prayer meetings and so on, but never with enthusiasm. We were in a capital city. I had a lot of other friends both ex-patriate and Ethiopian. What did it matter if I wasn't getting on with the other missionaries? I was really quite astonished when the more senior members of the group suddenly turned on me and suggested that it might be better for them (for them, mark you, not me!) if I left the Mission.

In the resulting clear-up, one thing stood out in my mind. God is interested in the bad relationships, not the good ones.

I had kind of worked out in my mind that if I had nine people liking me and enjoying my friendship and company, what did it matter if the tenth couldn't stand the sight of me? That was his hard luck, not mine. But what I felt God saying to me at that time was that he was most interested in the tenth! The nine didn't cancel out the tenth: rather, the tenth spoiled the other nine.

So I started looking for, and trying to concentrate on, the tenth person in my life.

Can you look for the 'tenth person' in your life: the man or woman you feel you will never manage to love? Even when you know you are feeling in your heart the stirrings of spiritual love; when the hard shell of fear and defensiveness is beginning to yield to the softer influence of the Spirit, you think, 'But I'll never make it with so-and-so.'

So what do we do?

I suggest the first thing is to learn the secret of building people up rather than 'putting them down'. I should think that if anyone has the 'gift' of making people feel small, I have! I seem to know by instinct what it is in their lives that is out of tune with their spiritual profession. And I usually tell them and often hurt them very much in the telling.

It was my non-Christian psychologist brother who said to me one day, 'You know, Rhena, I think you probably do have insight into people's problems, but just remember: because you can spot other people's sore toes, you don't have to tread on them.'

That was quite a revelation to me. I had assumed that if I could see where other people were 'wrong' (often that simply meant 'not in agreement with me') then obviously it was up to me to set them right: lovingly, of course! But Don's remark put things in a different perspective. If we can see other people's failings (and most of us are a lot better at seeing other people's failings than we are at seeing our own, of course) then we should use that knowledge to *build up* and not to put down. And this should be very specially the Christian's task.

We are so threatened by each other, aren't we? And the minute we are made to feel inferior, we respond by saying something to make the other person feel inferior and every time this sort of interchange takes place a further strain is placed on the relationship.

Single people can have quite sharp tongues. (So can the married, of course, but sometimes they can get rid of it privately on their partners!) But sometimes I think the single learn sharpness because they are so used to being 'put down' by the married. When that happens they react by attempting to 'put down' the married and you end up with just the greatest relationship!

I think the picture of the 'good wife' in Proverbs 31 is worth studying by every woman, married or single. There is a lovely verse there . . .

'. . . and the teaching of kindness is on her tongue' (v.26).

I'm working on it!

Yes, the ministry of the Christian is to encourage and build up. 'Encourage one another and build one another up,' says Paul in 1 Thessalonians 5:11. Of course we have to do that sincerely.

I can still remember a friend who was visiting Addis Ababa. He was, for some reason, driving me across Addis, and all the way he told me how he thought I was doing a really great job as the Editor of the Christian magazine we published. By the end of the ride he'd got me feeling about ten feet tall. But he ruined it all by saying as he dropped me at my house: 'Well, Rhena, it's been great to talk to you. I've been feeling lately we need to encourage each other more than we do. I've been reading a book about it.'

I looked after him sadly.

So I'd only been an exercise.

Anyway, my first suggestion with the 'tenth person' in your life—after you have taken off the dust covers of course—is to assume that one of your problems with him or her is that one of you, or both of you, feels inferior to the other. And just in case it's him, build him up. Never mind if you think he's too big already. That may be just the outward man. *Build him up.* Look for things you like about him and tell him and others about them. When he's with you, concentrate on making him feel good and encouraged by your presence. (If it's you who feels inferior, then you'd better also have a go at building yourself up—try re-reading chapter 1 and 2 of this book as a start!)

My second suggestion is that you pray for him daily. Such prayers when first uttered may not be very sincere but they will become so. Somehow it's almost impossible to be sarcastic with God!

The third suggestion is to make quite certain that you are not *doing* anything to injure him or her. This means avoiding the temptation to make life harder for him in some way and not undermining him when you are talking with other people. It also means not reacting against *any* actions or words of his that appear to be against you. It's a question of really trying quite hard not to return evil for evil. 'An eye for an eye,' said Mahatma Gandhi, 'ends up by making the whole world blind.'

I'm not pretending that any of this is easy. I'm telling you how you can work towards releasing the flow of God's love towards someone you dislike!

Larry Christenson had some useful things to say on this in his book *The Renewed Mind* (Kingsway

Publications 1975). He said that it is up to the believer to put on the outward form of Christ and then God will work the inward change in the heart. We create the outward form of, for example patience or love, by a kind deed, by listening, by prayer and then we must have faith to believe that God will fill the form with the genuine thing. The secret of sanctification is to 'construct the outward forms of holiness with expectant faith that God will fill them.'

But we must work at it for we cannot afford to keep grudges in our hearts. To leave unhealed relationships in our lives clogs the channel and sours the water of God's love which can flow through us to others. At least we must be sure that we have done our part in making healing possible.

7 Healing the Hurts

I have spent so much time talking about learning how to love because I believe it is the key to a happy single life.

> And Jesus said to them, "Truly, I say to you... everyone who has left houses or brothers or sisters or father or mother or children or lands for my name's sake, will receive a hundredfold, and inherit eternal life" (Mt 19:28,29).

Yes, a hundredfold, as you let go your human family links and open yourself to the wider world of the family of God: and if you feel you'll never learn to spread yourself so thinly, here is some encouragement from Betty Pulkingham writing about her struggles in learning to live with her extended family:

> ...I'll never forget the day...when my thoughts screamed out to the Lord, "I can't love twenty people all at once!" And as I stood frozen in my own exasperation and defeat, the Lord spoke to my thoughts. "Very

well," he said, "try loving just one at a time. Try loving the person you're face to face with now." I looked up into the face of one of his dear saints and I was suddenly freed from the burden of numbers...free to love...one at a time...hour by hour...day by day." (Betty Pulkingham, *Mustard Seeds*, Hodder and Stoughton 1977.)

The greatest joy of a loving ministry is that your family is widened, never narrowed.

But—and there is nearly always a 'but' some-where—there are certainly some boggy patches around when we start loving people. I mentioned one in chapter five: the person we feel we'll never get to love. In this chapter I'd like to mention two more. The first is the hurt that comes when people we love reject us or leave us.

That loving people also means getting hurt is just a fact of life. Some people fear the hurt so much that they will not let themselves love. Perhaps we have been hurt so much that we're just not interested in letting anyone hurt us like that again. But we can't keep that up and still live a normal life. We are, as children of God, made for love and to love. To shut down that side of us is to invite spiritual and emotional death.

We have to live with the fact that love and hurt come as a package deal: for everyone.

I got hurt quite badly recently: by an African Christian whom I loved but with whom it appeared I simply could not form a working relationship. I shared it with a number of praying friends. Their letters in response surprised me and comforted me. 'I know what you're feeling…', 'I went through an experience like that…' and so on. It brought us closer together. I wasn't the only one who knew that sort of hurt!

Even God the Holy Spirit can be grieved (Eph 4:30); and Jesus wept over Jerusalem (Lk 19:41).

The hurt is even worse if rejection is involved. I have sometimes wondered if a wife or husband deserted by their partners did not sometimes wish the partner had died, rather than let them suffer not only the loss but the rejection as well.

The real questions are: to what extent are we incapacitated by the hurt, and how long do we lie flat on our face?

In Joshua 7 we read the story of the defeat at Ai. The people of God who had entered the promised land, who had seen Jericho fall before them, who had every expectation of great miracles ahead, had suffered a humiliating defeat. The hearts of the people, we read, 'melted and became as water'. And their leader, that famous hero of Jericho, Joshua, 'fell flat on his face until evening.'

Yes, I know what it is to 'fall flat on my face' and so do you and the odd thing is, we tend to want to stay there. It's almost easier to hang around grovelling in our hurt and self-pity than it is to get up and go on!

The Lord said unto Joshua, 'Arise. Why have you thus fallen upon your face?… Up, sanctify the people and say to the people…' (10, 13). 'Get up,' said the Lord. 'There are things I want you to start doing!'

Yes, the Lord will let us grieve, but not for too long.

'Stop the world' we cry. 'We want to get off!' But we can't get off. Nor can we stop. We have to go on, with our pain, and believe what everyone says: that time will heal. Not a set time, incidentally, but just time. What we must *not* do is to harden our hearts against loving. Loving means hurt but, and let me say it again, far far better have the love and the hurt than to have neither. If you hurt, it shows you are still alive!

To learn about the kind of love that can 'let go', eases the amount of pain we feel. The mother must accept that she has, eventually, to let her children go. The wife (especially the Christian worker's wife!) has to let go of her husband, often for months at a time. The single person has to let go friendships all the time. And 'letting go' is never very easy.

Single people who move around as much as I do, know what it is to let people go. You form relationships that mean so much but—in a few months perhaps—you are moving on, or they are. And each time you hurt. A dear African friend said to me once in Kenya, 'You know, Rhena. We're not going to grow old together!'

How wonderful the expectation of heaven is to me. No more goodbyes!

Let go. Hold things (even people, if you can) on the palm of your hand so that God can take them away without hurting you. An essential characteristic of the mobility that is often—though not always— one of the great advantages of the single ministry, is the ability to let go and go on without losing love for others and zeal for the ministry.

'For his sake,' said Paul (Phil 3:8) 'I have suffered

47

the loss of all things and count them as refuse, in order that I may gain Christ...'

Would that we could say the same.

The second area of difficulty is when a single person loves a married man or woman and, desiring that person in sexual fulfilment and possession, finds as a Christian that his or her love is frustrated, agonizing and a threat to their whole way of life.

The first thing to acknowledge, I think, is that the Christian who feels like this is operating in the realm of natural love rather than spiritual. It is natural love that thinks in terms of possession and demands fulfilment, against other biblical principles, not the love which comes from God through the Holy Spirit.

I have worked with many men whom I have truly come to love. Because I love them I recognize that, if they are married, they have 'another half', a wife. So it becomes important to me to meet her and their children because I will not really get to know the 'whole man' if I do not. My love for him, which leads me to desire for him the very best, spreads over his marriage and his family, and instead of loving only one, I have a family to love. And if this sounds incredibly naive to you I can only say that I speak from my experience and have come to love many families in that way.

But there comes a time when that does not operate because 'possession' enters into the picture, and when the last thing you want to do is to meet his wife or her husband! What then?

If you give in to it, as many do, then your spiritual life will become crippled. God's highest calling does not lie the way of sin, and you are putting your own self fulfilment before fulfilment as a child of God. I read an unusual rendering of Matthew 10:39 recently: 'If any man seeks his own fulfilment, he shall lose it. But if any man surrenders his own fulfilment for my sake and the gospel's, he shall find it.'

If you can overcome it, either by removing yourself totally from the scene or by letting your natural love be 'transformed' into spiritual love, then you may be in for a 'valley of the soul' but you will come out triumphant!

To love someone so much that you can honestly put their welfare before your own is not a disaster even if it leads you into both hurt and humiliation. It can be a healthy spiritual exercise!

To all who experience unrequited or unfulfilled love of this sort, and who have made it through without open sin, I would say 'be glad'. It tells you that you are still alive; it tells you more about the love of God. And rejoice that heaven awaits where love will never be wrong and always be fulfilled!

8 People-centred Living

To make a success of relationships in general is important to us all; and to the single person, who is possibly going to have a wider and more varied circle of friends than many married people, success may well be crucial to a happy life. So having spent so much time talking about love, I feel the need to spend a little time discussing what else makes a relationship successful.

Love has to be there, of course: it is the background and the basic ingredient of good relationships, but the behaviour that springs from it has to communicate love successfully to the other person. In other words, there has to be some wisdom around, some understanding of how relationships work out, and also some ability to translate love into action. Some of this comes from the ability to see individual 'persons' in your life rather than a number of people. Sometimes we don't achieve a good relationship simply because we don't perceive that there is a relationship to be made.

Keith Miller in his book, *The Second Touch*, takes his

title from the story of Jesus healing a blind man:

> And (Jesus) took the blind man by the hand and led him out of the village; and when he had spit on his eyes and laid his hands upon him, he asked him, "Do you see anything?" And he looked up and said, "I see men; but they look like trees walking." Then again he laid his hands upon his eyes; and he looked intently and was restored, and saw everything clearly (Mk 8:23–25).

Miller describes how he had been so involved with 'witnessing' to chosen people (as a 'Communicator' I would refer to them as my 'target audience') that he had not really taken notice of the ordinary people he met every day. 'For years,' he said, 'the people along my daily path might as well have been trees walking by me.'

He needed a 'second touch' to help him get things in focus. After this, he wrote:

> The focus of life was almost imperceptibly changing from the distant horizon of tomorrow or next month to the immediate present, the *now*...I had marched into the future looking straight ahead—passing by the unconsciously searching eyes of those people beside the road which I was travelling....Now, each day, each relationship, began to take on new importance. God might have something new to do in this relationship.... (Keith Miller, *The Second Touch*, Word Books: London and Waco, Texas 1967.)

I understood this. Without really realizing what I was doing, I had been dividing people into people-I-found-interesting and people-I-found-dull. The former I had cultivated, sought out, enjoyed; the latter I had hardly noticed. But somewhere in these past years there must have been a kind of 'second touch' on my life and the *people* I meet are much more *persons* to me now.

Yes, it might well need a 'second touch' for some of us who are given to dreaming dreams of the future to see separate *persons* in the people we meet each day: and to accept those persons with all their needs, value-systems, beliefs and experiences as important and significant in our lives.

But relationships are never easy and the whole business gets progressively more difficult the more unlike you are from the person you are facing. Safe in our Western middle-class ethic and life-style, we don't have too much of a problem identifying with each other. We are, together, motivated to buy any-thing from a deep-freeze shaped like a coffin, to the *Swisch Crunch Crackle* cornflakes with a *New offer of free rose bushes* on the back of the packet. We have learned how to dress appropriately, what to talk about at the Women's Institute, and just how to stop Mrs Jones down the street from being too friendly.

But once we step out of the circle in which we were born, we cannot be quite so confident. We can no longer interpret correctly the non-verbal communi-cation patterns of our neighbours and even their words give us problems.

America was something of an eye-opener to me in this respect. I assumed on arrival that at least I would be able to understand what they *said*, but I was wrong. It took me nearly a whole year to discover that a 'bum steer' was not, as I had thought, some kind of misshapen deer, and the first words spoken in my hearing at Wheaton College (from one student to another) are worth recording:

'Jeet?'

'No. Jew?'

It took me some days to translate this correctly as:

'Did you eat?'

'No. Did you?'

Yes, the problems in cross-cultural communication make the whole matter of achieving good relationships even more difficult!

But, on the other hand, involvement in other cultures can help us see some of the weaknesses in our own. The problem I mentioned earlier: that of overlooking the people we meet in our desire to get the job done, might be partly a Western trait. It is not seen so much in Africa and, in fact, it is from Africans that I have often received quiet rebukes in this matter.

'Debbie!' I used to cry, bursting in on my Kenyan secretary at eight o'clock in the morning. 'I forgot to ask you to type out these letters and I've lost the Tear Fund file and please make an appointment with Mr Kamau for me!'

Gracious as always, Debbie would take the letters from me, smile, and say politely, 'Good morning, Miss Taylor.'

Greeting someone properly in Africa matters a lot. The 'Hi! How are you?' of the Westerner who is around the corner and out of sight before you can open your mouth, is just not acceptable. And I will not easily forget the deep hurt and bewilderment which I saw in the eyes of an older African man as a white secretary in a modern, stream-lined office greeted him with the sharp words, 'Yes? What can I do for you?'

We laugh sometimes in the West at the lengthy African greetings, but I wonder if we should. A carefully given greeting is an acknowledgement that the other person exists as a person with his own needs, problems and family: an acknowledgement that, at that moment, *you* are in touch with *him* and you are important to each other.

Years in Africa have certainly made me understand that—generally speaking—we in the West are more product oriented than people oriented. We have our eye on the end result (answering our mail or 'winning people for the Lord') and sometimes we scramble over people to reach it. The African, more often, will have his eye upon the people he is relating to while he works towards that end result.

'Learn to disagree like an African, Rhena,' an African friend used to say to me. 'Don't confront people in public. Go and see someone you think you will clash with, in private, before the meeting, and come to agreement. Then the public meeting will end without bruised relationships.'

Hard advice for me who, a product of the West, see nothing amiss with a good verbal argument in a committee meeting!

But, in fact, I have to admit that the African emphasis on people before achievement is probably more scriptural than ours. And don't think we can get away with a kind of half-and-half focus.

Do you know this picture?

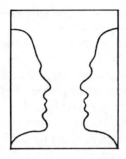

It is one I keep seeing in textbooks on psychology. Some people see it as a picture of a chalice or vase, and others see it as two people's faces looking at each other. One of the things it demonstrates is that we cannot really focus on two things at the same time. As you look at the picture you *either* see a vase *or* you see people's faces: never both together.

And I believe that in life we cannot manage to give priority to both people and achievement. We have to make a choice and that choice affects our whole way of looking at things.

For example, suppose you have, in Africa, a printing press and publishing operation started and run by white Western missionaries. It is well maintained and the printing is of high quality; it meets its deadlines and appears efficient in all respects. But the atmosphere is tense, the employees are neither relaxed nor happy, and there is ill-feeling between the management and the 'shop floor'. Then that printing operation is Africanized. Perhaps the general quality of the printing, in Western eyes at any rate, goes down, a few deadlines are missed, but the employees are generally happier and more contented. Now, has the standard of that printing operation gone up or down? It used to make more money, but is that how a Christian judges success?

When a committee meets, is it better to start exactly on time, or to wait while people chat and late-comers arrive? 'More business will get done if we don't waste time at the start,' we Westerners mutter. But will it? And is that time spent chatting really 'wasting time'?

This whole matter is complex, but I think that one way of making a success of relationships is to make them a priority. *People* should be important to us: more important than our jobs, our personal achievements, our life style.

The other suggestion I have to make in this chapter also relates to my experiences in Africa and picks up again the question of feelings of inferiority and superiority mentioned in chapter five.

Over the years I have observed that one of the biggest problems in the whole question of missionary/national relationships is the assumption that the white is helping, ministering to, or 'advising' the black. A workable relationship may be formed where this is the case, but not real friendship. Friendship is based on mutual need.

The fact that this happens in the missionary world is a result of the innate feeling in the West that we have it all and it is therefore our duty to impart it to the rest of the world. We must go to the poor, unfortunate third world nations and 'help them' get where we are.

A good look at Western society might make us think again. Do we really want others to be where we are?

In some respects, of course, we do. In others, it would be a lot better if we were where they are.

But it's hard for a young missionary going from the West to Africa today honestly to believe that.

'The gift we have to give to the rest of the world,' said a management lecturer in the US, 'is to teach it to manage its affairs.'

I was so surprised that I asked him to repeat it, which he did.

I was too timid to ask whether he really thought the rest of the world *wanted* to have their affairs managed for them.

The fact is, of course, that they don't, and, I say it again, real friendship will not be achieved in the context of one person 'helping' another. Successful and loving relationships are formed on the basis of mutual need.

One of my great friends in Nairobi is an African teacher whose husband went to the United Kingdom for a year or so to study, leaving her with three children. Though they had agreed to the separation, it was not easy for Julia to learn to live without John in Nairobi. About the same time I was struggling with being a woman alone in an unfamiliar situation. So we found ourselves getting together quite often: trying to cope with our cars alone and keep them on the road; dealing with household matters, praying together over problems as they arose and generally sharing our lives. That way a friendship began which has lasted over the years. It was a friendship based on mutual need.

I have heard missionaries talk about 'discipling' people and about their 'ministry' among the African people. And I find myself wondering if they have any friends! But to achieve friendship over cultural barriers is not easy.

A young couple struggled for two years in an African small town to fulfil their calling as missionaries and finally left.

'The only African relationship that I'm sorry to sever is with our dog,' said the husband as their lovely golden labrador found another home.

Don't condemn them. Many missionaries are in the same position.

I hear a lot said today about 'brotherhood' on the missionary scene, but what kind of response would you make towards your brother if he walked, uninvited, into your kitchen one morning and said, 'I've come to help you.'

Perhaps, if you were going through a period of special need, that might be acceptable. Otherwise you might well say, 'Thanks very much. I can manage, myself!'

You see, on the whole, brotherhood means sharing: just being together. Loving and being loved. Taking and giving.

Friendships where one is the giver and the other the taker, or one the helper and one the helped, are just not going to make it.

9 Single-minded Devotion

I have a friend who is now the senior master of a big comprehensive school in London. He had been promoted from a department head and I met him about a month after he started the job.

'What's it like?' I asked him.

'It's a lot more responsibility,' he answered, 'but I get to see an awful lot more of the Headmaster!'

Perhaps one of the special joys of being single is just that: it's possible to see an awful lot more of the headmaster!

Single people, in the normal way of things, have more time to spend in prayer and meditation on God's word than do the married. This is surely behind Paul's remark in 1 Corinthians 7 that it is the single who are more anxious how to please the Lord. Celibacy in the Roman Catholic church has always been highly regarded and surely it is for this reason. The single have more opportunity to be a Mary and sit at the Lord's feet simply because they don't have to spend so much time being a Martha; they can develop a clearer spiritual insight, a deeper knowledge of God's Word, a greater devotion to his service.

Unfortunately it is rare for the single person today

to accept that as one of the perks of being single. Bombarded by the cultural and social implications that to be unmarried implies a state of under achievement and unfulfilment, the single person is often driven into a life of activity simply to prove to others that they are popular, needed and fulfilled. They make sure they are seen as 'Marthas' because society tells them that the Marthas are the lucky ones.

'I hate the weekends!' I remember a single woman missionary saying to me in Nairobi. She was honest, at any rate!

But why did she 'hate the weekends'? Because she didn't go to work then and so had to find other things to do and because she had been brought up to believe that to sit alone on a Friday or Saturday evening doing the equivalent of 'writing letters and washing her hair' was just about the worse thing that could happen to her. If she happened to live with another girl who had been invited out, her evenings would be sheer misery. Time that could have been offered to the Lord was spent in self-pity and depression. But I suspect that it was the pressure of her cultural background that brought it about rather than what she herself really believed.

In the USA I learned about my 'peer group' and discovered that to reject your 'peer group' was tantamount to rejecting yourself. It was a bit difficult in my immediate circle in Nairobi to find a 'peer group' member: there were no other unmarried middle-aged missionary types around. However I eventually found one in another mission: Diana. She was about my age and was unmarried and I decided she could qualify as my 'peer group'. So, every three months or so, I looked her up: just to keep in touch with my peer group as the text books said I should.

Diana was just about as unlike me as she could be. She was far quieter for one thing, and had a much smaller circle of friends. She wouldn't drive her car at night, colour-wash her hair, or come and meet my friends. I just could not believe that someone who lived so retired a life could be happy, but my efforts to reform her met with no success and I suspect that the times I spent with her left her as depressed as they did me.

I was making the mistake of thinking *my* life style, simply because it was busier and had more people in it, was better than *her* life style. Fortunately she was strong enough to resist my efforts and I can remember the Lord saying to me one day, 'Leave her alone and stop criticizing her. She is made for one life, you for another.'

You see, I had made the assumption there about life that 'the busier, the better'. And I was wrong.

For most of my missionary career I had lived with other missionaries so when, in Nairobi, I found I would be living alone I was somewhat alarmed. I felt I had to be 'busy'. I made sure that I was invited out on my days off and my weekends, or I invited people in. And I suddenly found myself in confusion. I remember one Saturday especially. I had a fairly small flat. The sitting room had a family of Malawians in it with several children playing on the floor; the kitchen was taken up with Ethiopians preparing some of their national food for a party later that night; and

61

in the bedroom a distracted mother was nursing a sick child. A knock came on the door and it was a Kenyan friend who I knew was going through a time of personal crisis. Tears were in her eyes.

'Rhena, I must talk to you.'

There was nowhere to go. All I could do was leave the flat and walk down the corridor outside with her.

'Sarah . . . there's nowhere to talk in my flat.'

She burst into tears and ran. I followed, to see her car being driven out of the car park.

After that occasion I had to re-think things. This wasn't the right way to live my life. It was about then that I read the book I mentioned in the last chapter: *The Second Touch* by Keith Miller. He had things to say about how to live a 'natural-sized life' rather than trying to live your life according to other people's expectations. He said, 'I saw that I had always been living a life like a suit two sizes too large, hoping I would grow into it.' I knew what he meant.

I had, perhaps unconsciously, decided that since I was single it was important to have a 'ministry' to 'people' and so I had organized it. But my days were getting too much for me. What I had to do was to find a way of living my own 'life-sized day' not the kind of day I thought a person in my position ought to live.

So I stopped worrying about how I was to spend my weekends. I left it to the Lord and he did a much better job than I had done. If I was alone in the evening, then I was alone and I loved it! I can remember coming into the flat, shutting the door, and dancing around the rooms: 'Lord, we're alone together. Isn't that terrific?'

I found out that, if I made no plans for the weekend, then it left God free to show me his. People just came: not in crowds any more but in ones, twos, families. Because they knew I was often at home they could come knowing I could give them my full attention, or just glad that they could sit down and watch television or read the latest magazine. I made friends and found myself with a 'ministry' far beyond the one I had had when I had lived with other missionaries.

I think, as single people, we should love our homes and want to be in them. Yes, even if that means a bed-sitter in Fulham or somewhere. A sordid, little bed-sitter can shine with the love and acceptance of Christ sometimes in a way a huge house filled with a squabbling family cannot! If we are relaxed and happy to be in our home then others will be and they will want to share it.

There are some times, of course, where plans are better made in advance and what I say above does not preclude sensible planning. I decide where I am going to go for Christmas, for example, because I know I tend to get homesick then. There are other times when we know in advance that we would be better off with people, so we plan. But we do not need to plan our way through every 'gap' in our lives, for the Lord is better than we are at knowing what a 'life-sized' day should be like for us.

Once I had learned to turn over 'spare time' to the Lord; once I had discovered that I could 'sit at the feet of Jesus' as easily on a Saturday night as I could on a Sunday morning, the pressure to be busy came right off and life ran much more smoothly.

10 Not to Be Pitied

'I think my biggest problem about being single is that my married friends all pity me.'

The speaker was a young missionary attending the seminar I addressed in Addis Ababa last year.

I agree that to handle other people's views of singleness is difficult. No one likes to be pitied or made to feel in some way inadequate and unwanted. No matter how sure I am of my calling, I wince when an African housewife says to me in her 'African English': 'May I come and visit you in your lonely house?' And I instantly have a vision of myself sitting down to a boiled egg in an empty sitting room instead of being surrounded by a vociferous family.

But remember that difficulties in relationships arise when you make people feel *inferior* to you, not superior. If they feel *superior*, the chances are good for future friendship! So, if you feel others are pitying you, let them: draw them closer to you and hope that then they might come to understand you are not so much to be pitied after all! Don't reject pity. Accept it: for all it hurts is your pride and there's nothing wrong with that having a good jolt now and again. Use it to form the basis of a loving friendship.

I do believe sincerely in my calling as a single person but just because someone 'pities me' and says something like, 'What a shame you're not married,' I don't leap to its defence. Later, in the bond of friendship, I might try to influence them to see the place of a single ministry but if we fight the battle on every front we will very soon be in trouble!

I have a friend, a pastor's wife, in Africa to whom I am trying to explain this.

She had a tendency, when I was in her home, to relegate me to the status of her daughter because I was unmarried. This came out sometimes if I was in their house while she was entertaining and she would ask me to hand around the tea or do other small jobs, saying to the other women, 'Rhena is our adopted daughter.'

I accepted this for a while but eventually felt the time had come to try and help her to see the place of the single ministry. First I made her acknowledge my age. I think at that time I was forty-three and she was forty-four. Then I explained that, by calling me her 'daughter' and 'praying for a husband for me' which she had often done, she was really calling into question God's choice of calling for me.

Ruth is a lovely and gracious woman, much in touch with the Lord, and really struggled with the concept. I remember saying to her, 'Ruth, I am your sister in Christ, not your daughter. I'll do anything you want me to in your house, but as your sister.'

Yes, it is hard for the African society to accept that

singleness can truly be part of God's plan for a man or woman. There is simply no place in traditional African society for the unmarried. In some societies widows automatically become part of their brother-in-law's household. In other tribes 'extra' women become the third or fourth wives of one of the elder men. In the African view, women need the protection of a man and have no place without it. The coming of industry and urbanization has certainly brought the working, single African girl into being but the pressures on her to marry are still far greater than in the West. Even in the city there is usually nowhere for her to live except with male relatives and, if she does not marry, she has no recognizable future. The place of the single in the church of God, is something many parts of the African church still has to come to terms with.

One of the reasons for the pressure to marry in many non-Western countries is because it is a man's duty to give a grandchild to his parents. It is unthinkable that a 'house' should die out: it is owed to their ancestors to continue it.

I can remember a class of African theological students explaining this to me.

'We must marry and have a son,' they said. 'This is the way we take our place in society, the way we honour our parents, the way we are remembered.'

I showed to them Isaiah 56:3:

Let not the eunuch say "Behold, I am a dry tree." For thus says the Lord: "To the eunuchs who keep my sabbaths, who choose the things that please me and hold fast my covenant, I will give in my house and within my walls a monument and a name better than sons and daughters; I will give them an everlasting name which shall not be cut off."

But, of course, cultural heritages are not discarded because of a verse of Scripture! We must accept that it is very hard indeed in some societies to remain single.

I have known some single missionaries who feel that they have no credibility when they try to preach the Gospel to people who believe that only married people are fully adult.

'I feel no one will listen to me,' said one woman in her early thirties. 'I feel they are saying, "Who is this woman? Where is her husband? Where are her children? If God has cursed her with barrenness, how can we listen to her?"'

Possibly this is true: on the human level. It is perhaps particularly true in Africa where who says something is generally considered more important than what is said. But on the spiritual level another factor enters into the communication process: the Spirit of God. Our authority to speak is from God.

'...as men of sincerity, as commissioned by God, in the sight of God we speak in Christ' says Paul (2 Cor 2:17).

Men and women whose minds are open to spiritual things will hear us and receive what we say whoever we are. Men and women whose minds are shut and hostile to the things of God will *not* hear us, whoever we are.

A young African pastor was cast down because the old men in his church would not listen to his advice or accept his ministry because he was not married.

'They say to me, "When you have a son, then we will listen",' he said to me.

Several months later he did get married and in due time he had a son. But, as the months passed, I did not see him looking any less frustrated.

'What's the matter?' I asked him. 'Aren't the elders accepting you, now that you have a son?'

He said, 'One of them said to me last week, "Ah, when you have given daughters away in marriage, then we will hear you"!'

Those elders did not want to accept the ministry of that younger man. Whatever he did, he would not have been listened to. It was not really his status that was at fault, it was that the minds of his 'audience' were shut against his message.

When God wants to give a message through you, your single status will not stop it being heard.

The state of singleness as a calling from God may not be understood very well by people around us, especially in some non-Western societies, but the important thing is how *we* understand it. If we can find happiness and fulfilment in the single state, we can be a living testimony to the grace and enablement of God in a very special calling.

11   Free to Take Risks

I was in Communist territory and outside the permitted limits of my tourist identity card. The British authorities in the country had already let it be generally known that they could not be held responsible for British personnel if they travelled beyond the legal limits of their passes.

I had not ignored this warning lightly, for the Mission in which I had served for many years took such things seriously. But the course I was to teach was not a 'permitted' course and it had been decided by local Christians that it had to be held away from the capital city. There had not really been a choice. I could hardly say to the Christian pastors and elders who had had the courage to assemble, that I did not have the courage to teach them!

The road blocks were the biggest problem and we were just coming up to one, travelling on a country bus. I was accompanied by a local Christian, a man a little older than myself, whose documents were in order.

'This is going to be simple, Rhena,' he told me

cheerfully as we saw ahead the familiar barriers and cluster of vehicles. 'Usually they let the women and children stay in the bus and the men get out with their papers. They'll all think you're my wife—she often travels with me—so just stay put. Which sounded fine except that the first thing that happened when the bus came to a standstill was that a soldier with his machine gun got on the bus and ordered, 'Everyone out!' and nothing in his demeanour suggested he didn't mean women and children.

We got out, on to the dry dusty road and lined up facing the usual array of guns and soldiers. I stood beside Stevan but no one was talking and we did not even look at each other. What now?

The bus was searched and then they gestured to the passengers. A soldier was at either door conducting a brief body search and then carefully inspecting everyone's papers. In my bag was the only 'paper' I had: a tourist identity card which would instantly tell them I was out of the permitted territory.

Stevan, without even looking at me, went forward among the first. He was searched, his papers were inspected and he was on. And I was still standing in the dust.

There was no blinding flash of light from heaven, no voice in my ear or figure at my side, but there was suddenly a calm certainty as to exactly what to do. And I did it. I jumped the, mostly male, queue and stood near the soldier who was searching the passengers at the back door of the bus, pretending to search in my handbag. After a minute I looked up helplessly as if I could not find what I was looking for.

'May I get on?' I said in the local language.

The soldier glanced briefly at me, looking me up and down. He saw an uninteresting looking, tired, rather dirty, middle-aged woman and jerked his head. I was on.

And in that whole bus I was the only one who did not have his or her papers examined carefully.

I sat down beside a still-tense Stevan.

'My Mission doesn't like this kind of thing,' I remarked mildly.

'Nothing to it,' he answered airily. 'Don't you know the story of Peter and the angel?'

Now this is a small incident and I know that the 'Brother Andrews' of this life could multiply such examples of the Lord's care. But this happened to *me*. The Lord of Heaven who has the universe in his hand and billions of people to think about, looked down on one grimy, weary, single woman missionary in the middle of a desert and for a moment the power of the armies of God broke through the clouds and touched me: just to get me on a bus! And such moments are precious to me; they are worth living.

Being single has meant that I am free to take risks that I might not take were I a mother of a family dependent on me. Being single has given me freedom to move around the world without having to pack up a household first. And this freedom has brought to me moments that I would not trade for anything else this side of eternity.

Because I was single, I did not immediately flee the country when it became clear that my life was being threatened in Ethiopia when the revolution first took place.

Because I was single, I could take time off to work in one of Africa's famine camps even though I risked (and got) typhus in so doing.

Because I was single, I went when I was forty to the States to take another degree.

Yes, the single ministry can be a very special one. I am constantly astonished at the simple courage of the 'unwept, unhonoured and unsung' heroines of the mission field: the single women. Not many of them will receive the acclamation of the Christian world, but their names will rank high in heaven.

I can remember a woman who attended a writing class I held in Nairobi. The students were nearly all Africans but this one white woman attended. She was the kind of missionary I would once have dismissed as 'rather uninteresting'. As part of a class exercise she described an experience she had had in another part of Africa. In the account she wrote:

'After we had suffered at the hands of the soldiers, we climbed the hill and got away.'

'This is far too vague,' I told her casually. 'We need some details. This sounds as if you were raped.'

'I was,' she said.

I looked at her. I knew her and I knew her Mission. I had never heard any story of rape.

'I've never heard that,' I said in surprise.

'No,' she said. 'We decided it was better not to tell anyone. Only the head of the Mission knows.'

'But...but....' She had just been home on furlough. 'Didn't you tell your family, your prayer partners? Didn't they ask you what happened?'

'No,' she said. 'It never arose. Just once my aunt said to me, "Wasn't it wonderful how those soldiers didn't hurt you while you were kept in that place?" And I just didn't answer.'

I was silent. Not only had she gone through that, without sharing it, but she had come back to the same continent and put herself potentially in the same danger for she was not working in the comparative safety of the city which I was enjoying.

'For it has been granted to you that for the sake of Christ you should not only believe in him but also suffer for his sake...' (Phil 1:29).

I can well believe that to suggest that the single are granted opportunities of special suffering for the Lord, is not going to make the calling more appealing to you. Nor would it be fair to the great saints of God for whom marriage has—sometimes—increased their suffering for Christ. But there can be no denying that the single person can offer his or her life more freely to the Lord and can enter dangerous situations more readily: and so, perhaps, has a greater opportunity both to 'suffer for his sake' and to know a very special fellowship with him.

My career in one of the famine camps of Africa was brief and inglorious. Despite all the right injections I succumbed to typhus after only a few weeks. But it was an experience which left its mark on me.

We used to start work in the morning in the 'orphanage': a mud house bare of everything except wide wooden 'shelves' coming out at waist height from the walls. There slept some fifty or sixty children who had been found alone in the camps. First the ones who could still walk would come out into the sun. Some were strong enough to catch my hand and play a little with the workers who were ladling out the high-protein cereal that had arrived with me. Others were on the outskirts of the crowd, moving slowly on thinner limbs.

Then we would go inside. The windows of the house were small and even the bright morning sun did not give enough light to enable us to see to the back of the 'shelves' or underneath them. We had to take a powerful flashlight with us which showed us that the bunks and the floor space were not entirely empty. In one place and another lay little bundles of clay-coloured cloth, one or two stirring feebly, others quite still. In one dark corner a little bony child crouched, its sharp pointed knees by its head, its eyes staring without expression.

It was our custom to get the healthy out first and then deal with the rest.

We began to examine the little heaps of rags, coaxing those that might be able to walk, to come outside. Often I picked up a bundle, not even sure that a child was really there, only to see, in a moment, the open, sunken eyes, the drooping neck.

Of course we were doing what we could, but we had so little in those early days: no way of getting anyone to hospital, not nearly enough drip feeds. People were dying around us at the rate of twenty or thirty a day, even more, and the children were often the first to go.

My memories of that time are so many: a child of about twelve stretched out on the dried grass, her

74

eyes dull and staring, her body a covered skeleton only, her loins shrunk to two pieces of pointed bone, her tiny breast still rising and falling.

'Can't we do something? Can't we help?'

'It's too late,' the weary medical student told me as he knelt beside her. 'She will die tomorrow.'

The next day I could hardly bear to enter the hut. The child was among the five dead that morning. That was a 'good' day. Sometimes the number was as high as twelve.

Not only children died: so did men and women—crouched against the wooden palings of the feeding huts; lying in the wall-less 'hospital', which was only a grass roof to provide shelter from the burning sun; at the very gate of the camp. They often died in the foetus position, curled up on the unyielding earth. One woman died like that, holding in her hand a piece of the hard bread which was all we could make at that time. She had no teeth left with which to chew it.

There were no tears in that place of death and suffering. I only once saw them, when a thin claw-like hand clutched at my skirt.

'Please . . . my man.'

Her husband was crouched against wooden palings but his eyes were the eyes of the dead.

'Mother . . . he is dead.'

'Yes, yes, I know. He must be buried.' She dragged him away from the slime of his own filth and he fell stiffly on his side. She could not straighten the limbs and there was no water in which to wash him. But he was clothed in a pitiful strip of blanket.

75

'It's the blanket,' the woman said to me desperately. 'Please, great lady, let him be buried in the blanket.'

I looked at the thin, torn and filthy shred of cloth.

'Of course, mother,' I said gently.

'Promise me this. The grave-men are coming. Promise me!'

'Yes, I will tell them.'

'No, no. They will steal it at the graveside,' the woman said frantically. 'Go with them and see him buried, great lady, I beg you.'

Those in the camp were not permitted to go to the great lime-washed pits of the burial ground.

'Very well,' I said.

And as I left I saw two tears form themselves in the wrinkled eyes and roll slowly down that dry and withered cheek. They were the only tears I saw in the month I was there. The place, the whole situation, was beyond tears.

Experiences of this kind, which have been mine because I have had the freedom to seek them out, have made me an inhabitant of a much wider world than the one I was born into. I can never look in quite the same way upon that world again. Somewhere there is a God and an eternity which will make bearable the unbearable. My eyes must be on him or I am lost indeed.

12 A Liberated Lifestyle

'But,' you say. 'That's all right for you, called into this exciting life of travel in Africa and elsewhere. But I'm not called to that. I'm called to be a post-office sorter in Chelmsford, or a nurse in Manchester, or a secretary in Westbury-on-Trym.'

Are you sure? Single people, no less than the married, like to put down roots and it just may be you are putting them down somewhere where there is little need of your services. For a mobile life is, to some extent, a life of sacrifice.

I can remember a kind of emotional crisis in my life that occurred when someone gave me two pictures: quite large and heavy ones. It was just after I had had to leave Ethiopia and when I had no idea where I was going except that I wanted to study in the States for a time. And I had no idea what I could do with two big pictures. True, my parents had a home, but they also had plenty of pictures on the walls. I certainly could not take them to the US with me and, in any case, they were so heavy that I couldn't imagine that I would ever be able to afford to take them to

Africa, should I ever return there. Nothing in my life ever quite showed me how homeless I was as did those two pictures!

Yes, a permanent home may well not be an option for some single people but this is something else we share with Jesus.

'Foxes have holes, and birds of the air have nests,' said Jesus to an enthusiastic would-be follower, 'but the Son of man has nowhere to lay his head' (Mt 8:20).

'Here have we no lasting city,' writes the author of Hebrews, 'but we seek the city which is to come' (Heb 13:14).

It will not be a new thought to you that homes, possessions, even family responsibilities, can be a weight on us that causes us, like the rich young ruler, to 'turn away sorrowfully' from the highest calling of our God.

So let us be glad, if we are single and homeless, that we have no such possessions! We can develop the ability to make a home of where we are, whether it be one room or a four-bedroomed house. I sometimes think the reason that more women than men are called to the single state is that they are natural home-makers. I can remember a bachelor friend of mine insisting that he couldn't be bothered with drawers and cupboards in his room, he just wanted half a dozen tables: one for his clothes, one for his shoes, one for his books and so on. Well, *he* might have felt at home in his room, but not many other people did!

But we are so good at putting down roots. We like

the security of the boat, not of the water. In fact we're even a bit slow to rock the boat sometimes, let alone get out of it. But I would say to the single: keep mobile; keep willing to move on to new things if the Lord calls you. You have less excuse than the married for a static ministry.

I know security is a hard thing to renounce. Doors suddenly close behind you and you are left standing in a draughty corridor that appears to be leading nowhere. There is a strong temptation to panic, to fear what has not yet been revealed to you, to cling to the familiar and turn back. But that might be a way to miss the best the Lord has for you. Remember you are safe by the side of Jesus, so, if necessary, keep travelling!

There is a hymn I love with the words in it:

> 'Here in the body pent,
> Absent from thee I roam,
> Yet nightly pitch my moving tent
> A day's march nearer home.'

Each day is a pilgrimage, a piece of the journey we will never have to travel over again. Each night we are a little nearer 'home'. Don't start building too big a city. Stay in a tent; travelling is easier that way.

But even as I write this I know there are very many single people who would love to be mobile—to have a change of scene and ministry—but who are just not able to. Perhaps they are forced to stay near an elderly mother, or they live with their parents who need them or they are, themselves, ill and unable to do very much.

I have a friend, Joy, who is a doctor. She has managed to keep her job going but all her spare time for years has been spent in caring for her elderly parents. First she cared for both of them and now for her mother alone who is over ninety. Joy herself is now reaching retirement age. It was over twenty years ago that she said to me wistfully, 'I always longed to be a missionary doctor in India.'

I have another friend who is partially sighted. She lives alone in a not very salubrious housing estate in the industrial midlands and has spent her working life as a home help.

What of these and others like them? How can they use this gift of singleness that, I have said, opens the door to adventure and wide experiences, when they are seemingly chained to a humdrum existence which may well involve invalid diets and bed pans? Aren't they just wasting their lives?

Twenty years ago I felt I was wasting my life when I was sent into the wilds of Ethiopia: a little corner of the earth so lonely and so dusty that I thought I would never see anyone I could relate to again, that I would dry up, wither away, and soon be forgotten by all. And it was there the Lord taught me something about waste.

Thomas Gray, a mid-eighteenth century poet, had it right when he wrote:

'Full many a gem of purest ray serene
The dark, unfathom'd caves of ocean bear.
Full many a flower is born to blush unseen
And waste its sweetness on the desert air.'

A beautiful thing in God's world does not need human acclaim to justify its existence. It is enough that God's eyes have seen it. A beautiful life buried in North Staffordshire is still a beautiful life and a joy to the Creator. His own Son on earth never travelled beyond the boundaries of his own small and unimportant country, never addressed big international conferences, and apparently formed a really deep relationship with only twelve people. Large influential audiences, the public acclaim of others, international travel and wide experiences were things he repudiated rather than sought.

Then why do we sometimes measure the worth of a Christian life in those terms to the extent that we think those who never had them are somehow not as valuable to God?

God just does not operate as we do. Judged by *our* standards, his budget would never be met, his account book would never balance. A young Christian at the very threshold of what promises to be an influential and fruitful career suddenly dies; a young missionary who has passed all the right committees and trained for two years in a Bible training college, returns home after only four months abroad, with inoperable cancer; a child born of Christian parents who could give him every advantage of home and education dies suddenly without a known cause; yes, and a healthy, highly-qualified doctor, who could have done so much in the needy areas of the world, is tied at the bedside of one querulous old lady. Is any of this waste? Not by God's standards.

You see, we are back to seeing with our eyes rather

than with his. We are in danger of measuring something we call 'achievement' for ourselves rather than letting God's word be the measurement we use. God's will is sovereign and God's will is best even if we do not at the time understand it. Lives cut short are not 'wasted' for only God knows what those lives were meant to achieve. A missionary could have been taken six thousand miles across the seas in order to bring one soul to Christ. And a life given in service to another is never wasted: it can be as rich and as valuable in God's sight as the life of any world-famous evangelist.

Jesus made it quite clear that the 'firsts' in our reckoning were not his when he said: 'But many that are first will be last, and the last first' (Mk 10:31), which is as clear an indication as there could be that we will get some surprises when it comes to positions in heaven!

Do you find it hard to really believe this? Your life has seemed to you so dull, so uninteresting compared to your friends' lives and you think, in your lower moments, that it has passed you by?

One of the loveliest comments on death I have ever read was printed in a women's magazine: 'I used to think that dying was like leaving somewhere before the party's over. But now I realize that the party is really going on somewhere else.'

Do you think, friend, that you have somehow 'missed out' on the party on earth? You need not. The party's still to come!

At this point, let me say a word to those single people who wonder if their lack of a partner will be noticed even in heaven. Remember this: marriage is for earth, not for heaven (Mt 22:30). We will never spend eternity divided into married and unmarried; or divided into those who have lots of friends and those with none!

This may hurt the widow who sees reunion with her husband as one of the greatest joys of heaven. Will the reunion not take place, then, and if it does, will her single friend still be looking on?

Don't be afraid. Your love for your partner was a reflection of that perfect and wholly fulfilled love to be entered into when you reach heaven. When you meet him you will love him even more deeply and perfectly than you did on earth, but that love will equally be given to all around you. All the shadows of beautiful things on earth will be found complete in heaven: fullness of life, fullness of love, with nothing to spoil it for us. We can't imagine it, but then we don't need to.

We're heading straight for it!

13 Faithful Servants

I was sitting in a humble little mud house in Ethiopia eight years after the revolution which had overthrown Emperor Haile Selassie and introduced the military Socialist government. Since that time, life for Christians in the country had got progressively more difficult and many churches had been closed.

It was 1982. I had left the country in 1975 and not returned until then. So after seven years away I had had a lot of 'catching up' to do with Ethiopian friends. This occasion was one of them. Though the couple entertaining me were poor, their monthly income far below what the West would call subsistence level, they had put on a real feast for me and invited two or three of my other friends to share it with me. We had all very much enjoyed the meal and the fellowship.

When the meal was over, coffee was brought in little handle-less cups on a wooden tray. While we were drinking this, the husband cleared his throat and stood up, his head nearly touching the clothes that were, in the absence of cupboards, hanging from a roof pole. He spoke in Amharic, one of the languages of Ethiopia, for no one there knew English. It is a gracious language and he spoke it slowly and with dignity as befitted his position as a deacon in the Ethiopian Orthodox church.

'Miss Rhena,' he said, bowing slightly to me. 'I have something to say to you.'

I nodded solemnly. We had all been rather taken by surprise. After-lunch speeches were not the custom of the country: but he was the man of the house, with every right to make a speech if he wished. In that culture, to rise to your feet was an indication of the extreme importance of what you were about to say. Dressed poorly, thin to the point of emaciation, he nevertheless had a simple dignity, and we were all respectfully silent.

'Miss Rhena, you have come back to us in this country after being away seven years,' he said. 'During those seven years you have been serving the Lord in another part of Africa. You have been travelling from people to people; from church to church. Now you are here with us. We want to say to you that you are to us an example of a faithful servant of God. We know that you could have married and had children and stayed with them in your country. But instead you have taken us as your family, and given your life to be with us in the body of Christ. We want to thank you, in the name of our Lord Jesus Christ, for this service you are giving to God.'

Ethiopians do not say anything simply, partly because the Amharic language does not allow them to. The above is a brief summary of quite a lengthy speech, backed up by reference to the Bible which he held in his hand.

It took me quite by surprise. Nothing we had talked about during the meal had specially indicated that this had been in my host's mind, and yet, when he spoke, it seemed to be with the sincerity and authority of a prophet of God. I could only mutter 'thank you' afterwards.

He was poor, almost uneducated. He struggled to read even the Bible because of bad sight and his job was a minimally paid clerk in a minor office. Yet he had it right. He saw and understood the ministry of the single in a way in which I wish the Western churches did!

This gap in the teaching of the Western churches has badly hurt the body of Christ. Week after week marriage and the nuclear family seem at the heart of sermons, weekends, conferences and services. It is 'Christian family week'; it is 'Mother's day'; it is 'How to bring up teenage children'. Of course there are families with young children in the pews: thank God for it. But are there not also the single, the widowed, the divorced, the separated? Are they 'non-persons' that so little teaching is given on their situations and their special ministry?

Perhaps the most serious indictment of the church's reluctance to admit to the joyful and fulfilling calling of singleness, is the marriages that sometimes take place among Christian women in their late thirties— marriages which do not seem to be very sensible. Women, desperate as they see their child-bearing years drawing to a close, marry non-Christians, men much younger than themselves, or of a different race.

I have nothing against either late marriages or mixed marriages, nor am I implying they are all a failure, but in twenty years as a missionary I have seen quite a number of older missionary women marry much younger men of the country in which they were working and, although not every such marriage ends in unhappiness, a good many of them do.

Why do these marriages take place? Because often women feel that they just cannot face life unmarried. And would Christian women feel like that if they had been taught to see singleness as a proud and happy option for the Christian; if they had been sincerely and gladly welcomed into the family of God?

If you are single now I would ask you to believe you have been given (for however long) the gift of singleness. How will you use it? When I was a child I learned part of an Anglican catechism in the Westminster Confession of Faith which describes the 'chief and highest end of man' as being to glorify God and enjoy him for ever. I haven't found a better short statement of the purpose of life. But I don't think you will manage to do either of those things if you live your life tense and unhappy because there seem to be happily married couples all around you and you are alone.

You are not alone. You are a part of the army of God on earth, a 'missionary' in a troubled and tension-filled planet that is heading for its own destruction. Whether your particular place in that army is a quiet one ministering mainly to one or two people, or whether it is a travelling one which is more widely known it is still a ministry given you by God who is at your side, able to fill the skies with heavenly nuclear missiles to defend you!

How I have loved that story in 2 Kings 6 when Elisha's servant gets up early in the morning and sees the enemy with his army of horses and chariots all around the city.

'Alas, my master,' he cries. 'What shall we do?'

And Elisha says, 'Fear not, for those that are with us are more than those who are with them.'

Can you believe that, when your office, your home, your church, seem to be grey all over and your life goes on day after day with nothing to look forward to; when, if you *do* have a 'ministry', you'd really like to know what it is? Can you believe there are heavenly powers around you right at this moment able to lift you up to continue the battle for the Lord with joy and courage?

We need an Elisha to pray for us!

'Open his eyes,' prayed Elisha, 'that he may see.'

'And behold, the mountain was full of horses and chariots of fire round about Elisha.'

The hosts of God are here today: around you.

Do not resent what the Lord has chosen for you. Imagine the feelings of a parent holding his small child's hand as they cross a busy main road. Suddenly the child shakes free: 'I hate this road. Why do we have to cross it? I want to walk by myself!'

And at the very moment when we need him most, we sometimes shake free from God in a mood of peevish anger.

God has very often shown me that I am behaving

like a petulant child.

Once a job I had enjoyed was taken from me and given to another. I found it hurtful and, because I had been doing it well, incomprehensible. I wanted it back and told the Lord so. And he gave me a kind of vision of a parent walking along with a child dragging at his hand begging for sweets which the parent, who knows that in a short while the child will be having a good meal, is not providing. And it was as if the Lord said quite clearly to me: 'That's what you are doing, Rhena: begging for sweets, when all the time I have something far more fulfilling for you to do just around the corner.'

I wonder just how much of our time we spend 'begging for sweets'?

You see what *we* have in mind for our 'ministry' may not be what the Lord has selected for us. When I was wrestling with the problem of having to leave a job I loved and seemed specially able to do, I read the story of David's plan to build the temple of the Lord in 1 Chronicles 17.

David decided that a wonderful culmination to his highly successful life as King of Israel would be a temple for the Lord. I can see him thinking that obviously he was just the right person to get it built: he had the charisma, the money, the contacts, the ability. Obviously Nathan the prophet thought so, too, because, when David first asked his advice, he said, 'Fine. Go ahead and build it'.

But God thought differently and Nathan had to take back his words. Next day he had to return to David and say, 'Thus says the Lord: you shall not build me a house to dwell in.' And the job was given to someone else.

It was a familiar story to me but what I noticed for the first time was verse 10, later on in Nathan's speech:

'Moreover I declare to you that the *Lord* will build *you* a house.'

David had got it a little wrong. He had planned to build God a house: but the Lord had something else in mind: he wanted to build David one. This is, of course, using 'house' in two different ways for the house the Lord built David was the 'house of David' into which Christ was born. But let us note that the Lord had planned a far greater future for David's 'house' than the one David himself had envisaged.

But I'm glad that, in the RSV at any rate, the same word is used: because at that time I saw that story in terms of ministries. So often we want to build up a ministry for the Lord. Our intentions are all good. But it isn't quite the right way to look at it. We must understand that *he* wants to build *us* one: and we should let him. We will be happier, more fulfilled, and more fruitful if we fit into his plans rather than asking him to fit into ours.

Sometimes to find the Lord's ministry for us takes a little time but it's worth doing—and I'd like to share here a personal experience concerning this.

There was a time in my Christian life when I did quite a lot of public speaking at different meetings and in different churches. I discovered, quite early on, that I was able to speak well and to hold people's attention. All in all, I thought I was quite a gifted

90

speaker and others seemed to share that view. However, somehow I never felt quite happy about it, although I couldn't put my finger on what was wrong.

At Wheaton College, where I went quite late on in my missionary life, I became very interested in the teaching concerning spiritual gifts. Class discussions were always encouraged and it was really through them that I began to see that there was a connection between our ministry for the Lord and the gifts that the Lord had given us to enable us to exercise that ministry.

'But aren't gifts of the Spirit given just at special times of need?' I asked a lecturer once. 'Do you necessarily have special ones and keep them?'

He smiled at me. 'I think when God gives a gift, it's generally for good,' he said. 'If I'm the liver of the body of Christ, then I stay the liver. I don't wake up one morning and suddenly find I've been changed into the hand.'

It seemed logical.

So my ministry was going to depend on what spiritual gifts the Lord had given me. How did I find out what those were? Presumably I considered what I did best. But wait a minute. The lecturer in that particular class then went on to talk about natural talents. 'Natural talents,' he said, 'may or may not be transformed into spiritual gifts. We have to find out whether they are or not.'

This seemed to make the matter even more complex. If we couldn't find out our spiritual gifts by what we could do well, then how could we find them out at all?

Lecturers at Wheaton generally got full marks from me for their ability to talk around the subject without sounding as if it was easy. What I remember from the following discussion was someone's comment: 'Gifts can be judged by what happens when you exercise them within the body of Christ. If you think you have the gift of teaching then don't ask yourself, "Am I a popular teacher?" or "Do I prepare my lessons well?" but, "When I teach, are people *taught*?" If you think you have the gift of leadership, don't ask yourself, "Do I enjoy leading?" or "Do I have good ideas about what people should do?", but "Are people *following* me?"' (That made me smile. I could think of a number of times in my life when I had been quite a long way 'out front', exercising the 'gift of leadership'. The only trouble was, when I had turned around, no one was out there with me!)

Anyway, thinking out that concept was very helpful to me when it came to considering my 'gift' of public speaking. When I spoke, I was doing so to pass on the message of the Lord, but the message of the Lord was not getting through. After I had spoken, many people would come to me and say things like, 'How good to hear a good missionary speaker.' Or, 'The Lord has really given you the gift of public speaking.' Hardly anyone would say, 'The Lord really spoke to me through what you said.'

This, I realized, was really what had been bothering me over the years and, as I thought it out, I wondered if my 'gift of public speaking' was a natural talent that the Lord had not chosen to make into a spiritual gift. At the same time I saw that what the

Lord was *actually* blessing in my life were the evenings I spent chatting with people, the talks in my office with one and another, the visits I made. It was after these times that people would say (sometimes years later), 'Do you remember talking to us that evening? We went to Bible college because of what you said then.' Or, 'It was then that I decided to change my whole way of life,' or whatever it was.

Perhaps the spiritual gift the Lord had given me was that of counselling, not of public speaking.

Are you wondering why I am making such a big thing of this? It is because making that discovery was very liberating to me. It didn't mean, of course, that I never again accepted invitations to speak. Sometimes it obviously seemed right to do so and the Lord blessed it. But it did mean I no longer sought out opportunities to speak and so could concentrate more on the ministry that the Lord had given: that of one-to-one talks and visits, which the Lord continues to bless. It makes quite a difference to my leave-periods in England if I think like this.

Yes, finding the particular ministry the Lord has for us may take a little time and thought: but it is always there. The Lord has called us to service, not to unemployment (and I am not talking here necessarily about paid employment). There is no such thing as unemployment in the body of Christ. So search for and find your special ministry. Don't try to be the little finger one day and the foot the next!

14 The God of New Beginnings

I want to end this book with one of my favourite missionary stories.

A missionary couple (we will call them Kenneth and Anne) had been working in the African countryside for some years. Kenneth had been a curate in England and their work was to pastor and encourage the small widely separated Christian churches in the area. They were tired at the time of the story and depressed, although they didn't admit it, because their work was apparently bearing so little fruit.

One Sunday, in a little village church, Kenneth preached a sermon on the 'nature of the church'. After it, the elders of the church asked him, without warning, to take part in the 'testimony giving' part of the service. He could not refuse and, standing up, he told the story of how he had come to the Lord as a boy of sixteen, and later had been called to Africa.

When he had finished there was a dead silence.

Then an old, wrinkled man got up dressed in very shabby clothing.

'Yes, brother. But all that happened years ago.

What we want to hear is what the Lord is doing for you *now*.'

Kenneth stared at the old man. He knew he could pretend; he could speak the phrases which would come to his lips quite easily because he had heard so many other testimonies; he could smile brightly and say 'Hallelujah' in every other sentence but... but... would he be able to deceive these people?

The face of the old African Christian was very kind and he was looking steadily at the young missionary. And Kenneth sat down, covered his face with his hands and wept.

Anne came quietly forward and knelt beside him, her head bowed.

For a moment there was silence and then, one by one, the elders came towards them and surrounded them, laying their hands on them. One or two of them prayed:

'Lord, this your child has fallen and is for the moment out of touch with you. Restore him in Jesus' name.'

'Lord Jesus, have mercy on your children and help them in their weakness.'

'Lord, bless these your children and may your Spirit's power be seen mightily at work in them in the days to come.'

It was the wife, Anne, who told me this story and at this point there were tears in her eyes.

'When they had finished praying everyone was quiet,' she said. 'When we talked about it afterwards, we discovered that both of us had felt very ashamed. We, who were supposed to be missionaries, examples and teachers to the local Christians, had been shown to be weak and powerless. Neither of us wanted to look up. I think we expected to see pity, contempt. But when we did look up, the only thing we saw in the faces of those elders was love, real love, understanding and acceptance. For the first time we really saw them as brethren in Christ and could take strength and encouragement from them.'

People expect missionaries to be among the most holy of God's people. But I have heard one Christian leader say, after a tour around one mission area, that he had never seen so much back-sliding as he had among the missionaries he had visited.

Yes, all of us, can 'back slide', can lose the fresh, powerful and living testimony to the Lord which will help us live our lives in a way that is pleasing to him. And slowly then our lives dry up and wither: defences come up against others, and we are in danger of living a love-less and unhappy life.

There is a promise in Hosea 14 which says, 'I will be as the dew to Israel' (v. 5).

Poor wretched Israel, fast bound in sin, filth, impurities, injustices: rushing towards its own exile, deaf to the voice of the Lord. And the Lord pleads: 'If only you will return... I will be to you as the dew' ...the cool, refreshing moisture that heralds the morning, the new day, the fresh untainted beginning.

Praise God that he is the God of new beginnings!